CW01267501

Arka Dhyana
Intuitive Meditation

Srinivas Arka

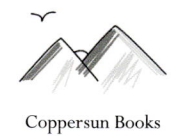

Coppersun Books

Published by Coppersun Books in the United Kingdom.

Copyright © 2013 by Srinivas Arka

www.arkadhyana.org

Srinivas Arka has asserted his right under the Copyright Designs and Patents Act 1988 to be identified as the author of this work.

All Rights Reserved. No part of this book may be reproduced in any form, by photocopying or by any electronic or mechanical means, including information storage or retrieval systems without permission in writing from both the copyright owner and the publisher of this book.

ISBN 0-9545418-7-1

Disclaimer

The ideas, procedures, and suggestions in this book are not intended as a substitute for the medical advice of a trained health professional. All matters regarding your health require medical supervision. Consult your physician about any conditions that may require diagnosis or medical attention before adopting the suggestions in this book. The author and publisher disclaim any liability arising directly or indirectly from the use of this book or of any of the procedures mentioned herein.

Author's Foreword

Arka Dhyana, also referred to as Intuitive Meditation (IM), which is a proven method, has been used with great benefit for over a quarter of a century by tens of thousands of people all around the world. This method has produced outstanding positive results in my own life and for sometime now, I have wanted to share it further with all of you who are now at last reading this book. Now with the book finally in your hands, I hope and trust that you will obtain a multitude of benefits from the practice of IM.

To expedite the evolution of our consciousness, we must not only develop a questioning mind, but also experience a soulful presence in the body, on the planet and in the Universe. To start with, we need to find answers silently within ourselves about who we really are. What is our true potential? Also what can we do to make a positive contribution to the world and to the development of humanity?

You are invited to read and experience these teachings for yourselves, with open minds and receptive hearts. In summary, I would say, that this book is a humble attempt to explain these difficult concepts, theories and practices as simply as possible without compromising the essence of each.

Throughout the book, words of guidance and encouragement, some of which are excerpted from my other published works; Intuitive Intelligence Programme, Petals of the Heart, Becoming Inspired and Adventures of Self-Discovery, appear to inspire your intuitive thoughts and promote a more engaged reading experience. If you are touched by these words, I encourage you to refer to the named works for further context and understanding.

*You are part of what happens outside, and what
happens inside you reflects in nature outside.
You are part of the whole. Your presence, your wellbeing and the
contribution you make to the world are extremely important.*

*Never undermine your role in the development
of humanity, in whatever the field.*

Whether it is small or big, it will add to global transformation.

Contents

Publisher's Foreword..10

A Note from the Author..11

Introduction...17

Consciousness..32

Beginning Arka Dhyana Intuitive Meditation 43

Breath 51

Sound 56

Touch 62

Arka Dhyana Intuitive Meditation: The Fundamentals 67

Nineteen Points: Positioning & Meaning 78

Customising & Progression 105

Arka Dhyana Postures: Quick Reference 112

Questions and Answers 114

# Publisher's Foreword

Arka Dhyana IM was developed by Srinivas Arka during many years of his own personal experience, study and research into the wider forms of meditation and its underlying philosophy.

In today's time-pressured environment and amid increasingly stressful lifestyles, the practice of this method can help you to more efficiently manage day-to-day challenges by learning how to redistribute your energy, how to relax in times of stress, and thereby transform stress into success.

It will also enable you to experience personal growth and further self development through the combined effects of breath, sound and touch. Most of us find ourselves juggling with life, trying to fulfil many different responsibilities. Stress does not come just from overwork, but also from monotony, the lack of a creative approach, or from having to work in a field in which you are not really interested. We need, in effect, to put the world on hold, to take time out to rest and recreate life, to explore new ways of bringing out our natural talents and skills, and even our innate knowledge and potential. So here is a way you can treat yourself to a precious journey of self-discovery in your own personal time and space.

Whilst meditating, you will discover the dimension of looking at yourself objectively as if you are an outside observer, a part of an audience watching your own performance. We need to extricate ourselves totally from the influence and opinions of others and also from our own entrenched perceptions, and take what might be termed an 'aerial view' of everything. From such a vantage point, we can see our whole picture with greater clarity. This can best be achieved through meditative practice.

A Note from the Author

The Invitation

With the dawn of this new century, people have started to become more aware of the Earth's health, its wealth, its beauty and its inseparable relationship with all species. We have also begun exploring the possibility of life elsewhere in our galaxy, the Milky Way, with a view to connecting ourselves more fully to it.

We may have the desire to know our true home and origins, in other words how and what we were, before coming into the world. We wish to remain ever youthful with a perfect body, to explore distant galaxies, to be present in many places at the same time, to be perfect in everything we do, and on top of all of that we want also to be recognised by others. These longings are all signs of the truth; we are not limited physical beings but infinite soulful beings with a greater role to play in the life of the Universe.

There is an invitation echoing ever more clearly from the valley of our intuition, one that invites us to explore more fully our mind, body, and soul. Fulfilment and complete answers cannot be found by mere exploration of the physical world. We also need to internalise our conscious awareness to become enlightened about the laws of the Universe through intuitive experience and evolution. Once we do this then we may embrace beauty, truth, love, the meaning of our presence and our relationship with all that surrounds us.

The Quest (India)

As a young boy, I noticed people who sat quietly with their eyes closed in the streets, parks and spiritual centres. I often wondered, 'What are they really doing? Are they tired, sleeping, dreaming, thinking or just too lazy to work?'

On the other hand, I was fascinated and felt that there was something special about them. I was increasingly drawn to watch them and to sit close to them.

The more I associated with these people, the more I noticed that there was a silent power, a grace and a mystique around them. Some spoke with illuminating insight after returning from a profound meditative silence.

Later I tried to meditate myself, thinking it was easy, and simply a matter of closing my eyes and just sitting still in one place. Yet, when I did it, I found that I had more thoughts, more images and more questions about everything around me. I also found myself asking questions such as, 'Why should we age? Why is youth not forever? Why don't we have wings? Why can't we walk on water? Why can't animals speak like humans? Why don't we have telescopic eyes to see stars? Will we ever make our home on the other side of the universe? Who lives amidst the stars?' As time passed, my quest continued; the same wondering mind became a questioning mind. I wanted to find answers to more serious questions and, day by day, the intensity of these questions increased significantly. I thought about disease, decrepitude, death, and the mystery of not knowing the past or our destiny. I questioned the meaning of life, the purpose of our existence and the nature and intention of this vast Universe. At this point, these bewildering questions turned into silent, powerful, deeper inquiry.

From that point on, I dedicated myself to learning how to meditate better and to finding what benefits could be gained from meditation. It took me a long time to research, study and experiment before I eventually gained insights, somewhat mystical in Nature, and of a clarity which was enlightening for me. This came in the form of experiences which bypassed the mind and led me to my innermost realms of the Self. This is when I discovered the power and potential of the humble heart. I realised that we were losing touch with our hearts and it was becoming difficult to connect with our deeper Self. I wanted to find a way to re-establish that connection. Eventually, the sum of these experiences led me to develop IM.

A humble heart is enough to resolve many problems concerning human relations.

Discovery of Key Points

At a very early age I was intrigued by one question above all others: Why did I feel a compelling presence and strength in some locations of my body? These experiences were not confined to one or two locations but happened in a rhythmic, wave-like movement without any conscious involvement of myself. After contemplating these points for quite some time, I gradually gained some control over them. Later I found I could consciously invite the experience to move to intended locations in my body. This seemed inexplicable and mystical at first, but with further meditation it became more of a spiritual nature.

The human body, I came to realise, seems to be a miniature reflection of the Universe and some key points in our bodies, in fact, have significance and greater connectivity to Nature and the Universe. By experiencing more of our presence at certain points, we can acquire particular knowledge, strength and connection with related forces in Nature.

As time unfolded, touch-sense became more and more interesting. This sense is the simplest mother sense. It is the largest sense covering almost the whole human body. Even if other senses become weak in bringing the outside data into the brain, the sense of touch will make up for the loss. In a way this sense is like a protective shield, which cautions us beforehand. It is tender in nature. It multitasks and is not just confined to the touch sensation. It eliminates sweat, takes part in temperature regulation and serves as an antiseptic agent. When you try to gain its understanding, it becomes complex. However, its experience is so real that it unambiguously pervades through the body as a special sense armour. It generates profound results when projected with our awareness, which is very magical.

At my speaking engagements, I used to tell the audience that touch sense would be explored and exploited in the coming decades. Sure enough, the new millennium has seen touch sense introduced as an integral part of modern life, on phones, computers, therapies, healing practices and more.

However, we live in a time characterised by a growing paradox: being in touch with humans in person is decreasing while keeping in touch via technical gadgets is becoming more prevalent.

Humans are losing balance. One of the effective ways of bringing an awareness of balance is through Meditational Practice, which is a deep contemplation on one's body, mind and spiritual Self.

Feeling the Sound: SAA-ROO-GO-VAUM

One day in Canada, as I walked in the woods in the early dawn hours, I experienced a strong pulse of sound coming from a remote space. In that moment, my whole body felt like a gong that had been struck by a sudden gust of wind. When you hit a gong, the impact of the sound is experienced, and then the rippling effect remains for some time. This happened to me rhythmically: striking and receding a total of four times. The last sound was VAUM, which was brighter than the rest and felt like rays of sunlight bouncing off my body and my very soul, and it left this extraordinary sound resonating in me for sometime. In the evening of that same day, I was scheduled to give a talk and there, I shared this sound in a singing tone. The audience joined the singing and found it to be very profound, healing and energising.

Gradually it became clearer to me that I should combine this sound with a sequence of my own touch to the body at nineteen locations. I began experimenting and as I did, I knew instinctively that these three elements—the SAA-ROO-GO-VAUM sound, the conscious touching of the key locations, and the conscious breathing—had the power to generate discovery of a thought body that is far more powerful than the physical or outer body.

*Make the Mind the meditator, the Soul the subject,
the Body the seat, the Universe the meditation centre.*

*Eliminating the distinction between these aspects
is the highest form of meditation.*

*If you sustain this awareness even for a moment, its qualitative
experience lasts longer, leaving you inspired and uplifted.*

Introduction

Over the centuries, many of the great sages and yogis have contributed to the concept of gaining greater control, especially the sage Patanjali, the first formal co-ordinator of yoga. Their intention and aim was to experience harmony between the soul, the mind and the body, as well as achieve the expansion of conscious-awareness in human beings.

Arka Dhyana is an Intuitive Meditation (IM) experienced at the heart level and is practised by combining three key components:

- ◇ Slow and conscious breathing.
- ◇ Singing and humming the sound *SAA-ROO-GO-VAUM*.
- ◇ A series of conscious, gentle touches at the nineteen key points of the body.

The whole sequence of breath, sound and touch unifies body, mind and spirit into an experience of undividedness, in preparation for the graceful descent to those inner realms which complement the physical, mental and emotional sides of our existence. The aim is not to control the mind, but to allow it to flow.

Mind is an extension of the deeper consciousness within us.

As the tail is to the comet, so is the mind to the deeper consciousness in the sky of our spirit.

Although specific techniques and steps are mentioned here, one can take the essence of Arka Dhyana and develop and evolve it in one's own way and still derive optimum benefits from its practice.

There are no rigidly imposed rules regarding time, location, duration, Asanas (postures), mantras or other external disciplines. However, certain necessary guidance is provided in this book. Arka Dhyana, used as a relaxation technique, may also help individuals to overcome stressful experiences by allowing them to relax more effectively. Additionally, this method can complement health by re-balancing your energies so that you can focus better and increase clarity of mind and heart.

Before you learn IM and begin to incorporate the practice into your life, it is beneficial to understand the key elements of nature, body, mind and inner consciousness, and then it will be easier for you to assimilate the philosophy of this method. *(The remainder of this introduction will attempt to discuss these elements in detail to aid in your study of the practice.)*

Realisation of Impermanence by Ancient Man

Human beings have always been on a quest to understand the true purpose of life. In the process of understanding and exploring life, ancient man minimised their requirements and lived an austere life, close to Nature.

They learnt that they had to resist all extra temptations towards mundane affairs, to conquer their minds at least. They may have felt helplessly sad knowing that the body is subject to growth and deterioration, aware of the inevitable infirmities of old age, the likely pains and sorrows, diseases, ailments and natural calamities that could befall them. It took a long time for them to realise that life is impermanent and youth is transitory; everything is subject to change and nothing seems to remain the same, except for who we really are deep down at the soul level.

On this intense quest for eternity and youth, there was no one to extract answers from, no text to read and no visible super-being with whom to communicate. The only option was to sit and meditate, which began with deep thinking and profound contemplation.

As a consequence, human beings found insightful answers to their silent inquiry. This encouraged them to put more of their heart and dedication into their further quest. As they refined this method of internal study and research, their learning became more disciplined and formally developed. Those who devoted themselves to solving some of the mysteries of life experienced illuminating insights and were recognised as philosophers, ascetics, teachers, yogis, saints and seers.

After a long labyrinth of this quest and the devotional paths of countless people, we arrive at where humans are today, with two ways of looking at our physical existence: One is to view it entirely from the perspective of science and logic. Another is to view it with the same intensity, but from a philosophical and metaphysical perspective.

Superbly intelligent Nature has positioned the heart in the correct part of our physique to align with emotions, in order to help us bring balance and reflection to what we think, feel and act. We need to increase our understanding and deepen our experience through both perspectives; heart-felt emotions and reasoning intelligence, so that we may become enlightened of infinite truth.

Mankind's Supremacy?

Humans are generally selfish in achieving their goals. In order to quench their insatiable curiosity about the world and beyond, they have encroached on both the animal and plant kingdoms.

Thousands of species have vanished in the last century because of unreasonable human intervention. Forests have been transformed into pastures, rivers polluted and deserts utilised for crop production. Humans have even begun to play a role as a geological force, levelling mountains, filling bays and changing the course of rivers.

As human beings, we do not seem to be more conscious or considerate about future generations. We are drifting away from the natural happy life that was taught to us by our ancestors.

Modern humans, seemingly oblivious to the cycle of evolution, are marching forward with a tragically blind awareness of the times. We have to progress, not by masquerading with a false economy down a negative path, but towards a path of light and joy. This becomes possible only through personal inquiry combined with a balanced approach to both the science of understanding external matter and the spirituality of experiencing energy within.

Humans are endowed with a rational intelligence that is higher than any other living entity on this planet. Although every entity displays specific congenital behaviour and characteristics, there are limits for them within their own existence and life structure. Animals, birds, reptiles and other mammals cannot effectively imitate the natural behaviour of any other creature. They do not have the ability to study and improve themselves intellectually, unless prompted by evolution. They can perform certain tasks if we train and guide them to awaken their potential.

On the contrary, scientific advancement, artistry, culture and society are proof of the manifestation of the creative ability and potential possessed only by human beings. The time has come for us to explore our inner world, in order to find an abundance that has not yet manifested in our exterior world. This is possible only when we embark upon an 'inner voyage' which is attainable by absorbing certain philosophies and practising meditations like IM.

The Universe is a mystical hologram.

For scientists, it is an Open University and research laboratory;

For poets, it is a place of cosmic inspiration;

For painters, it is a spacious enchanting gallery;

For philosophers, it is a cosmic riddle inviting many philosophies and theories.

Nature is stunningly spectacular and will remain so if we do not interfere excessively with it. We alone have the authority to rule over the world and we also have a great responsibility to ourselves and to all other living beings. We are endowed with privileges and facilities to care for the world and to experience its wealth and beauty. We could have been fully governed by cosmic laws, but we were fortunate to have been given the free will to execute our ideas and thoughts, although the results may not be entirely in our hands. What is certain, however, is that we at least have some degree of freedom within our capacity to exercise our will and thoughts.

The question now is how should we direct our efforts? Science is busy researching new areas to satisfy our unending curiosity. In the pursuit of this, our lives have become too mechanical and we have drifted away from a more natural way of living. We have advanced scientifically, to the extent that we cannot even imagine how our ancestors lived, yet the legacies they left still survived, even when we fail to take notice of them in today's rapidly changing world.

Our ultra-modern lifestyle has played a major part in polluting the natural, serene atmosphere of our lives and our planet. The harmful wavelengths of electromagnetic radiation are silently and directly bombarding us. This has already caused increased incidence of hearing impairment, heart disease, cancer, skin disorders and respiratory complications. Even plants, trees and animal species have not been spared this damage.

We now need more resistance to, and protection from, outside disturbances so that we can overcome this negativity in the environment around us. However, we cannot simply follow the traditional methods that were suited to the conditions, atmosphere and human nature that prevailed in the past. We must advance and expand our approach to include spirituality.

We possess the innate ability to judge right from wrong, despite the irresistible temptation towards material things. Our intuition provides strong impulses from within our own selves in times of greatest need, if we make an appeal to it.

Undoubtedly, we all have basic noble qualities, but have forgotten that we are born as enlightened beings. Each of us can be a 'scientist of the consciousness of the inner world', as those who have reclaimed their enlightenment remind us from time to time. We need to redefine our notions of time, as the 'beginning' and the 'end' are only relative terms on a cosmic scale. Everything on a cosmic scale seems to operate within its own cycle. The world is mobilised beautifully, not in a haphazard manner, but in a well-defined order.

Living Body and Soul

The living body is the physical unique container, the embodiment of essential life force. It is astonishingly well engineered and is aesthetically touched by Nature. It is your dwelling place, the genius of both Nature and Universe at work within you, perfectly blended opposites, a timeless soul in a time-bound body in perfect balance.

The soul, the subtlest entity, is also the hardest to define. The concept of the soul can be extended to any living entity. The soul is beyond our quantitative perception and yet it simultaneously has all the qualities we can ascribe to it and more. The soul can be imagined as both infinite and smaller than any known particle in Nature.

Mind

The mind is an entity constructed within the living conscious brain - which can be influenced by the bodily condition, and vice versa, without which we cannot communicate with the world or have an awareness of our own existence. It is hard to distinguish yourself from your own mind.

To understand the mind, we have to compare and contrast it with the brain. By itself, the brain has no ability to think or react, so we may question what is behind the mind-brain duality. Inquiries such as this gave birth to the refined concept of 'mind'. This concept was first used to describe the theoretical force that maintains our rhythmic bodily functions and was believed to pervade the body. Later, this wonderful concept branched out into more defined terms such as intelligence, thoughts, self, soul, consciousness and so forth.

The brain can be treated as purely physical, but the effort to separate mind from brain is akin to separating an object from the space it occupies. The body, which is purely physical and comes under our own physical perception, is a quantitative body. Although the brain is the main centre for controlling the body, the brain cannot function alone. It requires a force or a life-current to regulate bodily functions, which enables the medulla (the breathing centre of the brain), to regulate the breathing system. We may call it soul, inner self or vital force.

Subliminal Mind

The body is physical, tangible, and palpable, while the mind is subtle. The subliminal mind is even subtler.

The subliminal mind is another layer of mind existing beneath the thinking mind, it maybe called sub-mind yet it is more resourceful from the thinking mind itself. The subliminal mind holds day to day information perhaps in more detail, not causing burden on the thinking mind. This layer of mind is more aware of the need to extend timely coordination with the body from secretion of hormones and chemicals to automatic reflexes and responses.

Medical science may not know exactly where the seat of consciousness lies, yet it is believed that the main centre for mind-consciousness is located in the reticular function of the brain. As most of our activity is subconscious, this could also be called the 'subliminal mind'.

Intelligence

Intelligence is an advanced ability of the mind to perform in quick-time, based on memory and reflex; intelligence is the ability to respond in a timely and appropriate manner.

The intellect is the ability to identify and deal with abstract concepts. Intelligence is activated by an inner urge, and depends on the experiences and knowledge you have acquired since you began to express your curiosity. Both memory and concentration are essential components of intelligence. When an object is heated, it releases the energy possessed by its molecules. In the same manner, when the mind undergoes a thinking process, thoughts emerge. When this process is more refined and advanced with recognised responses, it is called intelligence.

Thought

Thought is both a creation of the mind and its essential property. Animals are not just instinctive as they surely have thoughts too, perhaps at a different level. If animals did not have thoughts, survival would become very difficult. When a snake hunts for its prey, it has to plan and make sure it will obtain its food. Birds must have thoughts in order to plan and prepare their migration, to breed, and later to return home.

The speed of thought could be faster than light. When you think about someone, you may be in their thoughts at that same time. Only certain people respond to you immediately by contacting you or by speaking about you with others. If they are seriously occupied, then pulses of your thought are picked up and stored by their subconscious mind. These are later retrieved by the surface-conscious mind or thrust forward in their dreams. This is likely to be the way that mankind will communicate in the future.

Philosophy of the Mind

Mind lives within the body and simply becomes non-existent with the demise of the body. The laws of the mind co-ordinate with the laws of the physical brain; both of these laws are equally important.

Higher understanding and enlightenment are possible through the metaphysical quest, and through spiritual experiences with meditation at their heart. It is not possible to achieve higher understanding and enlightenment through mere debate and logical reasoning. The mind is an entity that makes the brain think and react. The mind appears prominently in the brain with the presence of whole Consciousness, and vanishes with the absence of Consciousness.

Try the following experiments to help you understand how the mind behaves when our senses are subjected to different stimuli:

Look at a small flickering light and then look at a steadily glowing bright light. A small flickering light draws our immediate attention more readily than a steadily glowing bright light. A simple reason for this is that there is a change at irregular intervals and the absence of light becomes obvious.

Although you know that you have a mind and you are in the mind - you also know you are different from it. Still you find yourself in a difficult situation to separate yourself from your mind. Once this is realised and experienced, then you can do many wonders.

Whilst watching a programme on television, close your ears with the palms of your hands. You still hear a humming sound due to vibration caused by air pressure and the air in your ears becomes hot with the warmth from your hand. As your ears no longer receive external sound vibrations, the eardrums become calm and sensitive to this humming sound. After a few seconds, look at what is on the television screen. While you were attentive to the humming sound, you were not aware of the visual images on the screen. When you begin to watch attentively, you do not hear the humming as intensely as you did before.

Now experiment and aim simultaneously to watch the pictures on the television screen and listen to the hum. Continue for a while until you get the feel of it. Notice how the mind oscillates from eyes to ears. This is easier to experience than to explain.

The absence and presence of the mind becomes very clear in the experiment above. So it may be said that the mind is only experienced as a subjective fact and not as a general belief, yet it is difficult to describe clearly. Whenever and wherever you give a command, the mind is ready for action in a flash. However, the brain has its limits when assessing split-second commands and movements of the mind.

Due to its unique nature, the mind cannot be compared to anything that exists in this Universe. It should not be mistaken for the brain, or the intellect, as it coordinates all of these. The paradox within this is that you may be the mind, but certainly the mind is not your full identity. It is a self-concept that grows with the body and with life experiences; the mind evolves with time. It may appear to be independent, but the mind is not. It is part of your soul and whole consciousness.

The Birth of the Mind

Humans were not aware that they had minds when they first came into existence; they discovered this during the process of evolution. In ancient times, our ancestors would have contemplated in solitude, perhaps questioning their own existence, or how the Universe was created, or the laws that governed living and non-living matter. They probably found it insightful and enlightening to make a silent profound inquiry within the depths of their soul. This process we now call 'Meditation' or serious self-pondering.

Senses

The senses are tools or instruments mainly located in the facial area of the body, each having different capabilities to enable us to interact with the world outside. The senses are uniquely differentiated from each other. The senses allow us to gather data and process responses to external stimuli.

Although we have five senses with which we perceive the world around us: taste, touch, smell, sight and sound, the mind cannot be present in all the senses all the time. The mind can only be present in one sense at a time. We have all had those moments when, despite looking, we did not fully notice something because our minds were preoccupied. Senses are merely instruments, but 'you' are the one who sees and hears. Only when you engage the mind can you see and hear, and when the mind is deeply occupied inwardly with some subject or object, the senses gradually recede in a subtle way, so that you become less conscious or less aware of what is happening around you.

There are many senses that enable us to experience the world; some are not yet known to us. Our senses are like gates, through which information enters and brings us awareness of different kinds of inner feelings and sensations. We appear to perceive the world mainly through our five senses: touch, hearing, taste, sight and smell.

The eyes are highly sensitive to the radiation of light. Even so, a human being can still function without sight. A cane becomes an extension of the hand for the purpose of 'feeling' for the uneven sidewalk or any other obstacles. Because of touch, people with visual impairment can communicate through Braille.

The eardrum receives the subtlest vibrations. One may be unable to hear, yet live a normal life in the hearing world. A deaf person may 'hear' music through their feet by feeling the vibrations coming from the floor.

Life would be less interesting if we could not taste food. Taste occurs when minute particles touch the taste buds. We can then perceive and differentiate the subtle differences between the tastes: sweet, sour, bitter and salty.

Smell and taste are very closely integrated; whenever you have smelled something strongly, it means you have almost 'tasted' it.

The body is like an industry. The brain is your Head Office.

The mind is your secretary. The heart is your home.

The soul is omnipresent throughout the body.

The mind can serve you effectively, once you have understood its nature well, resolved conflicts within you and mastered it through heart level inquiry, experiencing the deeper self through meditation.

Consciousness

The State of Being Conscious

In human beings, consciousness manifests as awareness. This is also true of plants and animals, but their expressions of awareness are different from those of humans.

For instance, plants show their awareness by responding to music with improved yields of fruits, flowers and crops. Humans also have this awareness in abundance.

A person is said to be conscious when they can be aware of what they are sensing, including processes such as thinking, seeing, hearing, feeling and imagining. When a person is conscious, they experience their surroundings. An absence of consciousness is observed when a person is in a deep coma; all voluntary physical and psychological activities have ceased, there is no alertness, no response to outside stimuli and the brain activity is minimal. They can remember hardly anything after regaining consciousness.

We experience heightened brain activity when we anticipate danger or threat; it is a primary quality of being conscious. However, we cannot be in this state

Consciousness has layers, as many as our thoughts.

all the time. Nevertheless, although we may not be aware of it, we are also responding and reacting subconsciously.

Some psychiatrists and psychologists may view the degree of consciousness as resulting from the activity in a special part of the brain, called the 'Reticular Activating System'. In keeping with this view, at any given moment, this part of the brain determines whether a person is drowsy, asleep, awake or highly alert and conscious.

However, in a deep experience of IM, you may appear to be unconscious in the physical sense, but internally you remain subtly, yet profoundly, conscious. You understand and respond at a higher level and it is possible to find solutions, answers and guidance that can be remembered after returning to the normal state of consciousness.

When considering this duality, it is important to note that unconsciousness should not be mistaken simply as a complete lack of awareness or as being in a state of a coma. The deeper meaning to the term unconsciousness is a level of consciousness that lies beneath our thinking-mind. The term unconsciousness can also be extended to inner consciousness, which is a repository of innate knowledge distinct from others and contains the essence of impressions of all that we have experienced in life. We are largely driven by this metaphysical faculty of the soul.

We can derive maximum benefits out of this amazing dichotomy through inward philosophical inquiry, expressing active compassion to the world and nature, and through meditational practices. Sometimes we naturally experience this phenomenon when we are deeply sad about a situation which causes us to withdraw from the outside world. It can also be experienced when we are extremely immersed in an emotional situation, causing a connection between consciousness and unconsciousness to form immediately. After this experience, which is spiritual in nature, you become a much clearer, guided individual and emerge with a brighter mind. Although being in this state may not last long, its inspiring positive impact will stay with you for a long period of time, particularly when it's recognised and acknowledged.

Humans can experience their existence profoundly when they are in a state of full awareness and consciousness. This awareness is re-established only when a person is able to understand and feel the presence of other living entities. This gives birth to ordinary intellect, which is common sense combined with basic awareness. This develops so that it becomes refined intelligence, built on logic and experience, which rationalises events and actions. The cultivation of rational and logical approaches sharpens our intelligence, which gradually becomes one of the most powerful faculties of consciousness that can perceive, assimilate and acknowledge abstract concepts and ideas. This is not adequate, we need to include spiritual practice, self-reflection and meditation for overall expansion of consciousness.

The deep-seated unique core consciousness of each individual impels humans to search for truth, love, meaning and deeper experiences of their purpose and potential.

There is a deep unconscious intuitive awareness, which transcends the domain that exists between our consciousness and body (usually termed Soul or Self). Through this awareness, one experiences pain and pleasure through mind and matter. With time, one yearns to achieve enlightenment on the journey of life. Anything we identify as part of our being is simply an extension of that Self/Soul, unconscious to our minds.

One's personal spiritual development means experiencing one's spiritual self, manifesting in our bodies and minds, via the heart. This happens through dedication, practice and recognising growth, and also by becoming consciously aware of one's evolution. This is an adventure of self-discovery, eventually leading to a fulfilling experience.

Consciousness and the Brain

The human brain is unique. It can decode complex information processed by its various subordinate centres. Advanced development of the cerebral cortex distinguishes human beings from animals. Cortical function is impossible without the co-ordination of sub-cortical centres. Diseases of these centres interfere with the transmission of impulses, this in turn will be reflected in disorders of the mind. Consciousness makes it possible for the individual to be aware of what passes through their own mind.

Medical science may not know exactly where the seat of consciousness lies, yet it is believed that the main centre for mind-consciousness is located in the reticular function of the brain.

When emotions, thoughts, feelings are compressed, they settle at the bottom of the subconscious mind creating pressure. Some thoughts later resurface in dreams. If emotions, thoughts and feelings are not released, they may cause severe damage to the cells, tissues and nerve centres, which could lead to a nervous breakdown, mental disorders or result in the harmful secretion of histamine or other chemicals.

One way to relieve emotional pressure is to create counter-emotions and thoughts that can dilute the effect of those thoughts that are causing great concern.

If you want to reach the core of your soul, you have to leave the realm of reasoning, and gracefully let yourself be soaked in beautiful experiences of being the extension of the universe. Then your senses and thoughts become less obtrusive and you are able to perceive the world through your deeper-feeling consciousness and glide into the timeless, intuitive and emotional landscape of your infinite inner being.

Consciousness as an Entity - Levels of Consciousness

Consciousness manifests itself through physical matter. Similar to bacteria that are able to survive with a complete lack of oxygen and in high temperatures, consciousness lacks boundaries, can take any form or shape, and can emerge under challenging life conditions. In spirituality, consciousness is mainly a non-physical, yet powerful entity that is the pivotal point of all life and activates the senses in every living being. It is highly responsive and expressive, and has many levels, especially in humans.

The 6 Main Levels of Consciousness

M (Mind) - Consciousness: Mind is the first level, which manifests on the surface of the cerebral region. As it becomes sharpened by the cultivation of learning, it evolves into a faculty called Intellect.

SM (Subliminal-Mind) - Consciousness: The second level, which is below the surface mind, is the subliminal or subconscious mind. We are unaware of its potential and capabilities, which may seem incredible to the surface mind. Many of your daily activities are governed by your subconscious mind.

F (Feeling-Mind) - Consciousness: The third level is the feeling mind. This feeling-consciousness generally prevails in the heart area and can thus be called the Heart or Heart-Consciousness. It includes an emotional faculty called intuition. Almost all mothers have this faculty naturally available and readily accessible to help them understand the intense needs of their children and people they care about.

H (Emotional-Heart) - Consciousness: The fourth level is the deeper heart, where you feel emotions with even greater intensity. This can be called the spiritual heart, or your inner consciousness. The presence of the surface mind is reduced, but the presence of the subliminal or subconscious mind is enhanced. It is formed by impressions gathered through all you have learned and experienced, along with the imprint of your personality.

HS (Heart-Soul) - Consciousness: The fifth level is between the deeper heart and the ultimate essential being (Soul). Here you experience inner-space, and the mystical Universe, where the laws of physics start reversing and lead you to experience many alternate realities and possibilities that give access to your own soul. Here you become more connected with Nature and the forces of the Universe.

PS (Pure-Self) - Consciousness: The sixth level is core consciousness. This is the very essence of your whole presence and of everything that you feel, think and do. It is addressed as the Soul or Self.

The different levels of consciousness within can be experienced via the inner voyage of IM, but much dedication is needed to explore one's inner Self.

In between these named levels of consciousness, there are many other levels that may be impossible to explain, as our vocabulary is limited. As you descend deeper from the surface mind, the experience becomes increasingly metaphysical and even mystical.

The reason for undertaking the process of re-experiencing the purity of our consciousness is to endeavour personally to reverse the evolution of all that has happened to us from the time of our birth to the present. We travel from the mind, to the heart, to deeper consciousness. This can be called 'The Journey from Rational Mind to Emotional Heart to Pure Consciousness'.

Who undertakes this internal journey? It is our ego, which is the fountain of thoughts, of the memories and emotional impressions that form our personality.

This journey leads to self-discovery and realisation, resulting in personal enlightenment. This is a state of heightened consciousness, which brings clarity, inner peace and the ability not just to understand the deeper meaning of life, but also to feel it. As your heart blossoms, you experience streaming compassion, empathy and intuitive wisdom.

In this state of consciousness you will be able to access most invaluable higher information related to life and elemental forces involved with your existence, connecting with the universal consciousness.

Awareness

Awareness is the effect of consciousness. If consciousness were a flower, awareness would be its fragrance and the brain would be the stem. You can cultivate awareness over a period of time by wilfully allowing it to flow or work in a specific direction, and can thus increase your knowledge of a subject. Everyone has the potential to raise their awareness in any field they desire. Sometimes they develop it on their own through self-learning or by formal education, or they may be motivated or helped to progress by someone who has already raised their awareness. There is currently a trend towards increasing awareness of health, the environment and spirituality.

Conscious Awareness

Conscious awareness takes one to an even deeper level. It is not just a matter of raising awareness intellectually through knowledge. Here you raise your awareness emotionally and with the full involvement of your deeper mind prevailing in the heart region. In this process you gain positive energy, intuitive wisdom and a sense of direction. It is not logical but one can experience it mystically - an inner reality which has the potential to become an outside reality. Some people may be conscious but are not effectively aware of their particular presence. Some are aware on the surface but not consciously aware because their emotional heart is not involved. Raising conscious awareness can be long lasting. Raising awareness merely on a certain issue of life may not be sustained for long, as it needs to be nursed from time to time.

Dwelling in your mind alone will not help you progress much.

You have to involve your heart in your thoughts, words and deeds.

The real reason for Meditation should be an inner, spiritual journey, with the prime goal of self-realisation.

First the mind heals itself, then the body, which leads to an increased Intuitive Awareness, after which many positive results follow.

Beginning Arka Dhyana Intuitive Meditation

Arka Dhyana IM is a way of connecting the mind, body and spirit through your heart via conscious-breath, sound and touch. It is an introduction and an invitation to experience deeper levels of your presence.

This is a heart level, intuitive and natural meditation. It is a journey of your 'I-Conscious Awareness,' from the 'surface-ego-mind' (the rational mind), to the emotional heart, to the pure state of enlightened consciousness.

This method helps us to feel revived and refreshed as our consciousness expands, leading us to greater awareness. Many people around the world have gained courage, improved their health, achieved heightened consciousness, and experienced peace and personal growth through the practice of this method.

Possible benefits:

- ◇ Reduced stress and anxiety
- ◇ Improved body functions

◇ Increased patience and self-confidence

◇ Further developed intuitive consciousness

Our Mystical Existence

An important precept of Arka Dhyana philosophy is that human consciousness recognises itself, and distinguishes itself, from matter, energy, space, time, light and material life.

Energy is constant, but its forms of manifestation are variable. The body is both matter and energy, while the spirit is 'self-governed conscious magnetic energy'. The body belongs to the solar system, the inner self belongs to the cosmos.

The physical body has layer upon layer of subtle forms, which provide a shield of protection around it. The spiritual body dwells in the physical body and extends beyond the physical body in an elliptical outline, as a magnetosphere, just as light in the bulb would extend itself through the body of glass.

In the early stages of IM, the first focus of your attention is the body. Progressively, you then experience the mind as another layer of the body, then the emotional layer and many others in between. Eventually you reach the touchless spiritual self, which is above the understanding of the rational mind and the perception of our own senses. That is your metaphysical existence, the foundation of your physical existence.

It is possible to feel your true and unique presence, when you are away from the bombardment of everyone's thoughts. We can experience and connect with the infinite power of the cosmos and this can awaken our own positive potential. In the atmosphere of silence and solitude, while experiencing Nature, we can feel our profound presence in many places and in many ways. The great progress achieved by mankind materially has brought increased physical comfort to people. However, it has also brought restlessness, lack of fulfilment,

Developing intuitive wisdom, re-establishing a deeper connection with Nature and finding inner peace becomes possible through a metaphysical approach, especially by raising conscious awareness through personal inquiry, altruistic service and meditational practices.

stress, as well as an absence of love and affection, amongst individuals, making life very complex and uncertain. At this crucial juncture of time, humanity is transiting through by raising many great loud questions that have never been asked before, showing inclination towards meditational practices that can help individuals to raise their conscious awareness for peace, health and progress.

IM is a natural and positive way to explore ourselves and our minds with a heart-centred approach. By consciously allowing your heart to supersede the mind, the mind will gracefully accept the new guidance as there is a convergence in our consciousness between the mind and the heart. Here, you experience natural insights and transformation.

Dhyana and Meditation

Dhyana cannot be translated simply as meditation, since it has a much deeper meaning. However, as there is no exact term in English to convey the total significance of Dhyana, the word 'meditation' is used.

A few decades ago, the term 'meditation' had a deep meaning, but it seems over-used today. For some, meditation is an art of controlling and enhancing the power of the mind. For others, meditation is merely a stress-relieving and health-enhancing mental exercise. It is also used as a substitute for prayer or supplication. However, in this instance 'meditation' is a clue that can help us consider Arka Dhyana in its essential purity.

Here, you are not meditating on some object or person; instead, you meditate upon your own deeper self, because this is where your highest wisdom unfolds.

Arka Dhyana is a Sanskrit term, created to describe a natural form of meditation that takes place at the heart level. The word 'Arka' is added to distinguish this method from other meditation systems. In Sanskrit, Arka means 'sun' and symbolises Soul and enlightened clarity. 'Dhyana' means 'to contemplate' or 'meditate with the involvement of your heart'. Patanjali, the sage of Yoga, mentioned in his treatise 'The Yoga Sutras' that there are eight limbs of Yoga: Yama, Niyama, Asana, Pranayama, Pratyahara, Dharana, Dhyana and Samadhi. Dhyana means experiencing fulfilment with profound conscious awareness. Arka Dhyana encourages individuals to experience and explore their inner selves at their own pace, in their own time and space.

This method focuses on awakening our unique, heart-centred, inner nature which enables us to experience the deeper mind, heart and inner Self. It is a gracefully adventurous, yet mystical process that raises self-awareness.

Every organ of the human body has its own significance and importance in giving us a certain shape and functionality for life on Earth. We establish a deeper connection with the body through our own conscious touch, breath and sound. Our language is currently too limited to explain this experience and we are still far from discovering the full matter and magic of the body.

Much of our existence is predominantly centred in our heads and we feel very little of our presence in other areas of our body. We often dwell mainly in the cockpit of our head and try to pilot our whole life's journey with little or no conscious awareness of our deeper spiritual presence. All too often, it is only when we experience pain in the body that we become negatively conscious of that region and try to offer it a healing touch.

With this method, you are inviting your mind, with your will and endeavour, to connect with different regions of the body. If you can feel your presence strongly in the nineteen points mentioned in this method, then you can feel wholeness. This will lead to a deepened spiritual inquiry and realisation, as well as to many other incidental physical benefits, beginning with health. In other words, we begin to experience a life of transformation.

The Effects

This method will enable you to develop the ability to transcend your thinking mind, which is currently consumed with the socially-programmed belief system of thoughts and logic, so that you can directly experience pure consciousness and realise your innate perfection.

You can become recharged, empowered and inspired and when that happens, you will feel positive. Some people have everything that they want in the material world, resources, money, position, family, a good house and most physical comforts, but still they do not feel happy. As they acquire more physical comfort, paradoxically, they often undergo discomfort and can even experience depression. Too much or too little physical comfort causes discomfort. You need clarity, vision, direction, sound health and above all inspiration to feel really good.

Stress and Relaxation

Relaxation is very important in today's busy world. Positive feelings are wholesome and healing, while negative feelings are disagreeable and can result in harmful secretions by certain glands, causing agitation in the nervous system, raising blood pressure and heart rate.

Stress has long been shown to have harmful effects on metabolic activity. The concept that imbalance of mental activity leads to physical illness is a very old belief.

A person in deep thought, or a reader, uses more energy than those who perform manual labour, because prolonged mental activity is more tiring than physical activity. The mind cannot be fully dissociated from the normal living body because it is an integral part of our physiological functions, which are in turn dominated by our state of mind. It is believed that the brain separates feelings into negative and positive coded impressions before storing them. When negative thoughts increase, our experiences will also be unpleasant, causing stress.

Some people resort to sedatives in an endeavour to ease their tension but these may offer only momentary relief and can lead to health problems. Physiological functions may appear normal but the individual feels an underlying stress that cannot be diagnosed unless psychologically observed and analysed. Some people become permanently addicted to these drugs and this ultimately contributes to weakening the social stability of their communities.

Strenuous activity stimulates the brain to increase its output of endorphins. These are opiate-like chemicals that produce a natural 'high,' and one acquires extraordinary physical strength when the output of these increases. In excess, these chemicals might also cause nervous disabilities, such as anxiety disorders that are harmful to normal health.

One can experience bliss through meditational practice. It has been observed that during meditation, the heart and respiratory rates become slower. In most cases, blood pressure is also lowered and the practitioner feels extremely relaxed.

Living Responsibly

Modern civilisation proudly boasts about its advances in technology. We have evolved and developed our minds to have a more logical and scientific approach so that we understand everything around us, including ourselves.

Science is continually inventing new gadgets to satisfy our never ending needs and desires in a promise to make our lives more comfortable and fulfilling. In trying to achieve its goals however, it has made life too mechanical and we have drifted away from natural living. We investigate everything, how it functions and why. We are largely interested in increasing our understanding of the physical side of life and exploring it.

This has often resulted in serious consequences and irreparable side effects, both to us and to the environment, including plant and animal species.

Free-will shapes our visions and thoughts, and influences our management of the environment. With such power comes great responsibility for all living beings. We have the abilities needed to care for the world and experience its pristine quality. However, we should question whether we are exercising these for the benefit and progress of humanity, the environment and our planet.

In today's loud and challenging world, we need more resistance to, and protection against, outside disturbances so that we can overcome the negativity around us. At the same time, we are also compelled to advance and to expand our approach towards our inner journey. This is spirituality.

Many people are now using meditation in an attempt to find inner peace, reduce stress and to improve health. There are many forms of meditation to achieve these goals. Each individual has to choose what is suitable for them.

Breath

Moment to moment, energy comes from breathing.

Every living entity breathes. We humans are endowed with the ability to carry out deep conscious breathing. However, it is not possible to do so all the time because we are occupied externally. In contrast, fast-paced intense deep breathing is not healthy. Therefore conscious breathing can be exercised when you feel the need to refresh yourself, or to unburden some of your stresses.

When breathing out, the air we exhale differs to the air we inhale. The air we inhale gets absorbed by the body, whereas the air we exhale is not recycled by our lungs. Thus this exhaled air is not chemically the same, nor does it have the same energy, as the inhaled air.

Slow conscious breathing can happen when you are sitting in an upright position, or even when you stretch or hear something melodious. It enhances the relaxation response and is therefore a vital component of relaxation techniques. Additionally, slow conscious breathing gives us a clue to the essence of real meditation. During conscious breathing, your respiratory rate and heart rate decrease, and blood pressure is reduced, resulting in a calming effect.

Go touch the heart. Draw the curtain of your eyes.

Inhale the beauty of Nature. Imbibe the truth and experience the energy of unconditional love from Nature.

*Exhale all that you want to unburden.
Celebrate the light of life.*

Life is one big wave of consciousness where there are waves within a wave, one long respiration. In between, there are millions of times we breathe unconsciously as an automatic response, and sometimes consciously. By becoming aware of the mechanics and the subtle nature of your breath, you will be able to carry out activities much more efficiently, whether it is weight lifting, martial arts, sprinting or balancing your body.

When sitting upright or standing, take a long conscious breath, filling your lungs as fully as is comfortable. This should be held for a couple of seconds, and then slowly exhaled.

Through breath you can connect with your inner Self. Breathing symbolically reminds you of every moment, of every rhythmic pulse of the life-force. If breathing is understood and experienced, you can tune in to the rhythm of the body, with Nature and other living beings. Breathing is a natural act, both voluntary and involuntary, between the palpable body and the touchless spirit within. It is physical, yet mystical, and when consciously embraced in silence, it is a spiritual experience.

Controlling one's breathing means controlling one's emotion. Controlling emotion by controlling breathing is physical. Controlling breathing through emotion is a mystical experience. Forceful deep breathing may produce some temporary benefits but it can cause problems. However, letting everything flow naturally like a river, with only subtle graceful navigation, gives long lasting positive results, energy and inspiration.

Taking three slow, conscious breaths will increase your concentration and help you relax and withdraw your attention from the external environment. When breathing deeply, fill your lungs as you inhale, using the depths of your lungs, not just the upper portion. This stretches the alveoli, which are the small air sacs deep within the lungs, and increases the lung capacity. As a result, good oxygenation of the blood is achieved and the elasticity of the lungs is increased, which can also help alleviate chronic lung disease. Overall, this improves or assists cardiothoracic control.

Breathing through the nose warms and moistens the air as it passes through the respiratory tract. Take time to breathe deeply and inhale and exhale gracefully to your full capacity.

- ◇ By breathing correctly, you gain physical benefits.
- ◇ If you become conscious of your breath and follow its rhythm, you gain mystical benefits.
- ◇ If you become absolutely absorbed in your breath, it becomes very subtle and you acquire spiritual insights and experiences.

Understanding your breathing in depth can even give you a glimpse of tomorrow, since any events that are about to happen in Nature are indicated first in our breathing. This is also the case for any changes that may happen in the body.

The first indication of any illness is indicated in your breath. By breathing properly you can avert many potential illnesses. By carefully observing or studying the qualities of your breath, such as its pressure, temperature, strength, force and duration, you can gauge the condition of the body and predict a potential health hazard. Then you can start directing your routine, habits, diet and activities in a defensive or curative direction.

Act of Breathing

Breath is incredibly subtle and yet the most powerful element in your body, underpinning your very existence. If well understood and applied, it can manifest health, wealth, joy and wisdom.

Breathing should ideally be slow, calm and conscious. One complete breath includes an inhalation and an exhalation.

Prolong the inhalation and extend the exhalation according to your capacity and comfort.

On exhalation, expel all the air as completely and comfortably as you can.

When breath control is perfected, the body becomes light, digestive powers increase and internal purification and joy are manifested.

The magic of breath is that the moment we become conscious of it, our breath becomes a little deeper. This helps our thoughts to become settled. Emotion and breathing are interconnected and independent.

Sound

Humming causes vibrations that beneficially affect both our physical and our subtle forms. Humming produced in the back of the throat causes the thyroid and carotid body to vibrate and this triggers changes that stimulate the sinuses, the nasal structures and the olfactory system. During conscious exhalation, negative energies are eliminated from the system with the emanation of sound vibrations.

The humming sound vibrates in the mouth, tongue, palate, throat, nasal passage and head, as well as throughout the whole body. Humming also stimulates the different nerve centres to release healing energy, leaving you feeling healthy, energetic, and cheerful.

The nature and quality of sound depends upon our state of emotional-consciousness at the time. When we are immersed in our thoughts and emotions, the sound becomes deep, effective, curative and even transformational.

Sound travels at a slower rate than light. The body, which represents sound, functions slower than thought. Your thoughts are like the rays of your soul. Thoughts emerge originally from the depth of the soul as intuitive feelings, then are converted into thoughts which travel at very high speed.

Like a musical instrument anyone can play and produce the melody of experience in a unique way; so too this special sound has many positive experiences to offer, according to the way one wishes to operate this sound.

One of the reasons we become stressed and frustrated is because our mind runs faster than the speed and rhythm of the body. If you want to feel relaxed, reduce thoughts to a lower level through silence and meditation or go to naturally scenic spots such as mountainous regions. Then the mind joins in with the pace and rhythm of the body. The body has its own intelligence and sectioned consciousness, which is shared by the soul. When thoughts are reduced, the body drops back to a minimal function. The functioning of the body can be reduced even further, until the distinction between the mind and body vanishes temporarily. The process is meditative, relaxing and refreshing.

The right pronunciation of sounds will benefit you, others and even the environment that surrounds you. Almost all religions in the world utilise some kind of humming sound, which purifies the mind and the environment.

SAA-ROO-GO-VAUM

Having no explicit literal meaning, this sound bypasses the mind and directly enters your heart level awareness. Therefore, it will not distract your attention or create images while you practise Arka Dhyana IM. A word with overt meaning might divert your attention by awakening many pleasant or unpleasant memories, or by building up complex images, thus stimulating your mind more.

In order to derive greater benefits, one has to master the frequency and pronunciation with the guidance of an experienced instructor. As you say each syllable of the sound, try to end each syllable on a vibrating hum by closing your mouth. The melody must be maintained throughout the practice session. The volume of *SAA-ROO-GO-VAUM* changes from low to high as your hands ascend the body. Your fingertips are highly sensitive and can pick up these sound energies.

Sound	How the sound is felt in the body	Effect
SAA	Begins to vibrate at the umbilical region and moves up to the diaphragm.	Produces vibrations in the thyroid and the carotid body area, creating subtle changes there. During expiration, the mouth and the nostrils work one after the other to drive out the negative qualities from the system with the emanation of sound vibrations.
ROO	Begins at the diaphragm and travels to the chest.	Produces vibrations in the tongue, the palate and the mouth.
GO	Begins at the chest and ends at the throat.	Stimulates the logical brain.
VAUM	Begins at the throat and culminates as a vibration in the head and crown region.	Stimulates the sinuses, the nasal structures and the olfactory bulb and nerves. This humming also stimulates structures in the base of the skull such as the pituitary gland, which is a very important gland in the body. It controls the production of vital hormones in the body and influences the pineal gland, about which medical science knows little at the moment, but which holds a very important place in spiritual development. It is considered to be the location of the 'Third Eye'.

Singing the sound can have positive effects on the body. For example, while 'S' in SAA is pronounced, the carotid body is stimulated. The carotid body is a chemoreceptor that is very sensitive to oxygen variations in the blood. The following table shows each syllable corresponding to a different region of the body, and recommends how that syllable should be pronounced in order to produce the maximum effect. The original pronunciation of this sound is available on the CD *'SAA-ROO-GO-VAUM'.*

All sounds originate in a subtle form from the navel, then resonate in the vocal chords, reverberate in the head and then recede back to the navel. Ventriloquists can relate to this. We have lost this link with the navel so we do not feel sound in the way we should. By determined practice, we can revitalise this link and re-experience this process of sound. The word *SAA-ROO-GO-VAUM* has a significant effect on the body. It is like ultrasonic sound therapy. You should sustain your breath as comfortably as you can to prolong the singing.

Each of the four syllables in *SAA-ROO-GO-VAUM* represents a different stage of understanding and experience. The following text illustrates the philosophical understanding behind the sound. As there is no direct meaning, only the essence can be conveyed.

SAA represents the experience of the material world. By experiencing your strong presence you are indirectly experiencing the world as well.

Although we recognise our presence on earth in a physical form, we are not fully aware of our deeper presence yet. Most of our presence is felt in the head region, where the main senses meet. With conscious touch and the accompaniment of your own created sound energy, you can become profoundly and consciously aware of the energy points mentioned in this method and awaken their potential. You can transmit your warmth and bring your awareness to those regions, healing and enhancing them. Imagine that when you touch, the area touched is glowing with the light of your own spirit.

With regular practice, you can consciously project the feeling of your presence vibrantly in different points of the body. You can increase the energy flow to a specific region of the body in the way that you wish; this can help alleviate pain or discomfort in that area. This, in turn, can also contribute to the experience of the body, mind, emotional heart and ultimately, the underlying spirit.

ROO prompts the experience of our physical bodies. We can deepen the experience by descending into deeper layers of the body, even down to the microscopic level. The deeper we experience the consciousness of our own bodies, the stronger we become. We become highly energised, confident, increasing our inner wisdom.

GO is the experience of the mind, which is difficult to analyse and separate yourself from, as it is present throughout the body. This is like trying to see darkness with a flashlight or torch. Similarly, you cannot experience your mind by analysing it with your own mind. You need to activate your emotional heart. When you return to the mind, you can conclude 'yes, I was in a state of mindlessness,' which is a relief from the burden of always being constrained by the confines of the mind.

VAUM is about experiencing our spiritual consciousness. It is profoundly resonant, vibrational and blissful.

The resonance and reverberation of this sound is blissfully intoxicating and enhances the feeling of the objects of consciousness, embracing the self or spirit, and your whole presence.

The mind is part of our spirit and its existence is predominantly in the head; however, its presence is felt everywhere internally. A principal purpose of pronouncing *SAA-ROO-GO-VAUM* is to become aware of the many layers and extensions of our spirit, such as the intellect, heart, senses, subconscious mind and intuition. These have a deep, inseparable connection with our spirit.

Touch

Touch informs us of the texture, the temperature, the nature of an object and much more. It is an integral part of IM.

Our closest experience is physical touch, which is a direct experience and ongoing reassurance of our physical existence, and it is useful to establish the presence of things around us. When something touches us, then communication becomes complete, and as a consequence an epiphany may be experienced as new knowledge dawns. When we hear, sound vibrations have to touch (reach) our eardrums. When we see the world, light reflected from it should touch (reach) our eyes and stimulate the retina to send a message to the brain for interpretation. This creates a three-dimensional image and experience. Air has to touch us and fire is recognised by the touch of its warmth on us. This is also the case with water and even with thoughts and emotions.

You can develop the sense of touch and experience the world through it, whether or not the other main senses are active. As the skin and nervous system are made of the same tissue, touch can be called the primary, or Mother Sense. For instance, you can sense light because of the effect of its temperature on your body. Touch is universal and the fundamental basis of our awareness. However, we have taken this primary sense for granted.

*Touch is the Mother Sense to feel the world with;
to feel the hardest objects with the softest touch.*

Touch invites your conscious awareness and energies to rise to the surface from the deeper recesses of the body, and it feels like some form of light manifests in that region. You may not see it, but you feel the warmth, energy and magnetism as your presence revitalises that region with your own conscious touch. It is so comforting and unifying that you feel deeply connected with your deeper Self. Our own natural touch has innate powerful healing qualities and we must not neglect any energy centres in the body if we want the whole body to thrive and be consciously awakened.

You perform these postures almost every day without being aware. For instance, sometimes you stand with your hands on your waist or you rub your eyes when you are tired, or sit on a chair with your hands on your knees. When you are in deep thought, you may instinctively rest your face in your palms. Also, bringing your hands unconsciously to the chest, whilst referring to yourself, makes you feel your presence more strongly. When you lose something your hands may go to touch the crown of the head to console yourself. These are all everyday postures that we use spontaneously.

With regular practice, these everyday touches will become more powerful and effective and as you consciously deepen your involvement, wherever you offer touch you will revive and energise that region.

Touch, synchronised with breath and sound, instils a powerful magnetic force into each point of the body. Suppose you do not touch your face for a day or two and then see how you look and feel. When you resume touching your face, you can see how life returns to the surface. Through touch, you invite your mind, life energy and healing to the desired area of your body.

Everyone has an innate magnetic healing power. That is why, when you are in pain, your hands instantaneously and instinctively go to that area. Then you experience some relief and afterwards the healing power recedes to deeper recesses of the body. Only a few people realise this specially gifted natural ability and learn to develop it further. In this method, your latent healing ability is automatically rekindled and brought to the surface at your will and command. This will benefit you as well as others. It is vital to bring a sincere and open-minded approach to your practice.

We perform activities everyday where we casually touch our bodies, but we do not touch certain key centres in the body with our full attention. Another person's healing touch, or your own, helps you to reawaken these centres, enabling you to feel your presence in that area more strongly. This is how we benefit from massage therapies.

The body is the earthly receptacle that contains the immortal spirit. Although we live in the body, we have not recognised our presence fully. Our very soul makes us experience the world through touch, using the body as an instrument, but the soul itself remains touchless and ageless.

The body can accept and receive the greatest benefit from our own touch. When we touch each part, we are not only touching the surface, but also touching everything within. This rekindles our innate, curative power, which revitalises energy at the cellular level, harmonising the brain and nervous system.

When you are stressed or when your body is tense or sore, you may want a massage to revive yourself. When you accept someone else's touch, perhaps a mother's or motherly touch, you can feel more of your presence in your body. If you want to, you can test how touch can be touchless, by experiencing touch when you are not consciously or fully aware of the physical act of touch. Think or talk about your problems, or focus on something else when you are having a massage. You may find that you do not enjoy and derive its full benefits, because you are not consciously aware of your presence in your body, as you are not conscious of being touched.

Touch helps to release stored energy in the body. Through touch you can experience curative and magnetic energies. This kind of touch, in the practice of Arka Dhyana, helps you to advance into the higher levels of awareness. When you are harmonising the body, mind and spirit by synchronising sound, breath and touch, you will feel the unity of the elements and forces flowing within your body.

Photo shot in Fiji Islands during Sunset, whilst practising IM

Arka Dhyana Intuitive Meditation: The Fundamentals

Mind and Preparation

Often our mind can affect and disturb us, but it can also entertain and even enlighten us, if used properly. We should use the mind to our benefit to find peace and to connect with our deeper selves. How can we manage our mind? Firstly, we have to know its very nature. We have a huge amount of information stored within us from our life experiences, and this information is sensitive, and ready to surface. A single stimulation can awaken hundreds of images; the simplest event can trigger some incident that happened ten years ago or more. When we are dealing with the mind, we have to be careful in our approach. There is a natural and positive way to explore it.

In IM, the mind is not applied forcefully to gain control; instead you nudge it so that it flows better. You will eventually master the movement of your mind and once you can do this, you can withdraw or project your mind into the desired location. This will also help you to generate more powerful, effective thoughts and to connect freely with people, Nature and other living beings. Remember, once you pass through the threshold of the heart, you can reach the essential

The first experience of spirituality is inner peace.

Once that threshold is reached, many doors of matrix realities open.

soul, seated at the core of everything that you think, say, feel and do, which could mean self-realisation.

With your special touch, you are educating your mind to flow freely and to be in tune with your purpose.

Getting Started

You can practise IM at any time and for as long as your body is able to. It may take half an hour or so, and should preferably be practised in the morning and evening. The calming atmosphere at twilight is particularly conducive. Emissions of thought vibrations from you and others are reduced, so you are less likely to be affected or influenced by them.

Hygiene is also an important prerequisite. Rinse your mouth with salt water. Use only a small amount of salt in the water and do not retain it in your mouth for more than ten seconds, otherwise the absorption of salt through the tongue becomes too high. Sodium chloride is an effective deterrent to bacterial growth in the mouth. Oral hygiene is the basis of good health, whether mental or physical. If your mouth is clean, usually the stomach is clean; and vice versa. Consequently, you will have a pleasant mind.

Morning practice is essential because this is the time to wake up and enter the world of duties and responsibilities. You need to prepare your mind to make the right decisions, achieve the best in the least time, recall yesterday's incidents and events, prepare to grasp the facts, understand the feelings and intentions of others towards you and be aware of your surroundings.

Sometimes you can practise IM in the evening if you are not able to sleep or as you prepare to sleep. If you do not have enough sleep and rest at night, you cannot be very alert or agile the next day. Sleep is as important as wakefulness, and prolonged sleepless nights can endanger one's life. A body with complex physiological, oxidative reactions cannot remain completely at rest, but voluntary physical actions can be suspended for a few hours and the expenditure of energy can be reduced. Then the body automatically turns to involuntary functional systems that can absorb energies and produce an effect that helps you to sleep with mental poise.

There are lots of hindering factors to having a good sleep, such as physical pain, dreams and psychological disturbance. The state of your mind during the day depends on how much you can rest during the night. How long you sleep is not very important; it is the quality of sleep that is the prime factor. The position you sleep in, the bed, the atmosphere you create, the nature of the food you consume and the type of conversation you had before falling asleep are all important factors. Above all, your state of emotion plays a predominant role in putting you to sleep.

Key Steps in Preparation

Journeying through the body means symbolically journeying into the farthest reaches of the Universe. We should feel our deeper presence in matter, which is a feeling of in-depth unity within.

The touch points in IM cover almost the entire body. However, you can invite your mind wherever there is any discomfort to help relieve or heal it through this method.

Preparation plays an important role in the practice of IM. Although this may be practised at any time, your state of mind, emotions and physical condition need to be considered first:

- ◇ Choose a quiet location that is neither too hot nor too cold, and softly lit.

- ◇ Wear loose comfortable clothes.

- ◇ If possible, remove eyeglasses, wristwatches and heavy jewellery.

- ◇ Try to practise on an empty stomach if you have sufficient energy. If absolutely necessary, a small amount of pure juice, milk or light vegetarian food may be taken. Avoid stimulating drinks before you practice.

- ◇ Drink some water to moisten the throat and calm the acidic reactions in the stomach. This effect can be felt immediately in the brain, which in turn helps you to meditate.

- ◇ Before practising in the morning, you can do some simple stretching or light exercise to warm the body, enabling you to sit for an extended period of time.

- ◇ Sit in a cross-legged posture on a cushion to help protect your bones, facing East or North. Alternatively, you might like to sit on a chair. The back is held straight to allow energy to flow properly. Facing East or North enables the Earth's magnetic currents to flow most effectively through the physical body. It also relaxes the mind and revitalises the nerves with very little effort.

- ◇ Sit straight with your head up. Your spine is erect and relaxed at the same time, so that there is less tension and stress in your muscles. Although the appearance of the posture may be firm, your muscles should not be. Rest your hands on your knees in Gnana Mudra (as illustrated on page 104) with the palms of your hands facing down, as if cupping the knees. Close your eyes and relax your body.

- ◇ The moment you close your eyes, you are partially separated from the world around you. You can immediately feel that the energy radiating via the eyes redirected inwardly. As a result, the burden on the brain and eyes from responding to external stimuli is reduced.

- ◇ Do not worry about what to concentrate on. The aim of IM is to facilitate you to achieve a state of peacefulness. A specific procedure for beginners is necessary as a guide, but not for advanced practitioners. The steps here are designed to help you to meditate better. Use them as a structure to develop your own practice, if you feel the need to.

◇ In this method, your mind is tamed and channelled in a circuitous way. Even though you make physical movements at this initial stage, concentration and calmness of mind are still experienced. Let your mind wander, set it free. Feel a strong impulse within, which voices the thought: 'Deep down I am different to my mind'.

◇ Take at least three slow, conscious breaths, which will make you feel relaxed and enable you to withdraw your attention from the external environment to your internal environment and will also increase concentration.

◇ Your eyes should remain closed throughout IM unless for some reason you are disturbed.

Eight-point and Twelve-point Arka Dhyana

When you are learning IM, it may be easier to start with levels that begin with fewer touch points. For ease of practice, the following eight-point and twelve-point stages are suggested. These may also be useful if you have limited time.

Each syllable of *SAA-ROO-GO-VAUM* is sung in sequence at each touch point (one syllable at each touch point). See the Quick Reference on page 112 for the touch points. You will find the methods for the relevant posture diagrams are described on the following pages. Note that the syllables in the posture diagrams are for nineteen-point IM.

Level 1: Eight-point IM

Touch Point	Sound
Feet	*SAA*
Shins	*ROO*
Knees	*GO*
Thighs	*VAUM*
Waist	*SAA*
Navel	*ROO*
Abdomen	*GO*
Chest	*VAUM*

Conclude with Yoga Nidra, as shown on page 101.

The recommended minimum number of days to practise is eight, once or twice a day.

Level 2 : Twelve-point IM

Touch Point	Sound
Feet	*SAA*
Shins	*ROO*
Knees	*GO*
Thighs	*VAUM*
Waist	*SAA*
Navel	*ROO*
Abdomen	*GO*
Chest	*VAUM*
Shoulders	*SAA*
Elbows	*ROO*
Hands Together	*GO*
Throat	*VAUM*

Conclude with Yoga Nidra, as shown on page 101.

The recommended minimum number of days to practise is twelve.

Nineteen-point Arka Dhyana

This is the complete Arka Dhyana, with all nineteen postures.

Refer to the table below and the posture diagrams on page 112 and onwards for all the touch points.

Level 3: Nineteen-point IM

Touch Point	Sound
Feet	SAA
Shins	ROO
Knees	GO
Thighs	VAUM
Waist	SAA
Navel	ROO
Abdomen	GO
Chest	VAUM
Shoulders	SAA
Elbows	ROO
Hands Together	GO
Throat	VAUM
Mouth	SAA
Nose	ROO
Cheeks	GO
Ears	VAUM
Eyes	SAA
Forehead	ROO
Crown of the Head	GO-VAUM
Hands Together	SAA-ROO-GO-VAUM

Conclude with Yoga Nidra, as shown on page 101.

The recommended minimum number of days to practise is nineteen.

At each touch point, feel your connection to that part of the body, experiencing the harmony between your body and mind. Your body should remain stationary with each posture. Only your hands and arms move in a flowing and graceful manner.

There is no rigid rule that specifies one has to stay at each point for a specific length of time. You can remain at each point for as long as you wish, feeling the Yogic touch. For example, when you are moving from the abdominal region to the chest region, if you wish to and feel the need, you can keep enjoying the effect of deep conscious respirations. During the process of IM, if your mind begins to wander, increase the pressure of touch immediately and the mind will be re-engaged. The presence of your mind can be strongly felt at each specific point.

Now you embark upon a journey. Ascend the body with your breath, sound and touch.

Remember to express your gratitude.

Gratitude is a very noble quality.

*It enables you to develop empathy,
reach heights of self-awareness, growth,
well-being and fulfilment.*

Nineteen Points: Positioning & Meaning

Feet

◇ Place your hands upon your feet.

◇ Your hands should be relaxed, pointing downwards and holding the front of the feet. The thumbs should be on the soles of the feet.

◇ Keep your eyes closed and draw your awareness to your feet.

◇ Take a resting breath.

◇ Sing *SAA* softly. Try to conclude with a humming, nasal sound.

◇ Take another resting breath and feel your presence in your feet.

◇ Now feel the after-effect of the harmonious sound vibrations.

◇ Move your hands to the next posture.

Your feet are largely taken for granted. The soles of the feet mirror the entire map of your body and have thousands of nerve endings, yet they are generally ignored. Feet bear your weight, yet usually look younger than your face. Touching the feet means you are touching the body; by looking after your feet, you are also looking after your body. Therefore, feet require the first touch.

Shins

- Move your hands in a gliding motion to your shins.
- All four fingers are closed around the shins with the thumbs on the calves.
- Keep your eyes closed and bring your awareness to your shins.
- Take a resting breath.
- Sing *ROO* ending with a humming, nasal sound.
- The volume of your singing should gradually be raised as you ascend the body.
- Take another resting breath and feel your presence in your shins.
- Now feel the after-effect of the harmonious sound vibrations.
- Move your hands to the next posture.

With this touch and by concentrating and projecting the humming sound in this region, you can alleviate shin splints or pain, or strengthen the area by re-registering it in your subliminal mind (people with arthritis could also try this). This regions appears to be hard, but it is very sensitive.

Knees

- Place your hands upon your knees, cupping the knees.

- With your eyes closed, project your awareness to your knees.

- Take a resting breath.

- Sing *GO* ending with a humming, nasal sound.

- The volume of your singing should gradually be raised as you ascend the body.

- Take another resting breath and feel your presence in your knees. Now feel the after-effect of the harmonious sound vibrations.

- Move your hands to the next posture.

The knees connect the thighs and the lower legs. There is a great deal of energy stored in reserve. If the knees are not attended to, cared for and touched properly, you will not be able to transport yourself easily from place to place.

Honour your presence in both knee-joints with your touch. If you have pain or discomfort in your knees, this can help you to feel better.

Thighs

- ◇ Place your hands palms down on your thighs, with the fingers pointing towards the knee.
- ◇ Keep your eyes closed and invite your awareness to your thighs.
- ◇ Take a resting breath.
- ◇ Sing *VAUM*.
- ◇ Now take another resting breath and feel your presence in your thighs.
- ◇ Move your hands to the next posture.

The thighs can absorb stress coming from the upper body. Thighs create a good bridge between the knee joints and the body. Here, your hands can rest easily, creating a balanced posture.

Waist

- Place your hands on your waist, so that your hands grip your waist.
- Keep your eyes closed and beam your awareness to your waist region.
- Take a resting breath.
- Sing *SAA* ending with a humming, nasal sound.
- Now take another resting breath and feel your presence in your waist.
- Move your hands to the next posture.

There is abundant compressed energy stored at the base of the spine. Energy is released from there with each breath and exertion. When you are angry, a lot more energy is released, making you feel tired very quickly. Energy required for strenuous physical activity emanates from here. This is a very important junction of nerve-connections, which conduct electrical impulses. The spine, as a whole, is an extremely important part of the body, as it contains a multitude of neurons.

Navel

- ◇ Place your hands on your navel with your fingers pointing in towards your stomach.

- ◇ Keep your eyes closed and transfer your awareness to your navel.

- ◇ Take a resting breath.

- ◇ Sing *ROO* ending with a humming, nasal sound.

- ◇ Now take another resting breath and feel your presence in your navel.

- ◇ Move your hands to the next posture.

The navel is where we were originally connected physically to our mothers, when in the womb. From ancient times, the quality of deep sound is known to emerge from the navel. To experience this, and to gain good control of your voice, gently press your navel when you breathe out. Ventriloquists use this technique to project their voice.

Abdomen

- ◇ Place your hands on your abdomen with your fingers meeting in the middle.

- ◇ Keep your eyes closed and shift your awareness to your abdomen.

- ◇ Take a resting breath.

- ◇ Sing *GO* ending with a humming, nasal sound.

- ◇ Now take another resting breath and feel your presence in your abdomen.

- ◇ Move your hands to the next posture.

Although soft, this region contains many organs. Usually this area is warm, because strong and constant chemical, mechanical and electrical functions take place here. The element 'fire' is predominantly situated here and hence digestion is possible. As it is located some distance from your face, you are not disturbed by its intense fiery activity.

This area greatly influences the state of mind in a person. A good stomach means a good mind. If you have indigestion, a stomachache or a gastrointestinal disorder, you will find it difficult to concentrate on anything. You may become moody and upset, and may also become weak and tired. Touching the abdominal area reminds us to have self-control.

Understanding how every organ has its own mind, nature, function and contribution can help to fulfil your purpose and mission in life. As soon as you touch an area, the organ touched feels refreshed and consequently you feel positive.

Chest

- ◇ Place your hands over your chest with your fingers open and your shoulders and arms relaxed.

- ◇ Keep your eyes closed and focus your awareness to your chest.

- ◇ Take a resting breath.

- ◇ Sing *VAUM.*

- ◇ Now take another resting breath and feel your presence in your chest.

- ◇ Move your hands to the next posture.

Your chest is where you naturally feel more of your true presence and your true Self. The brain becomes recharged and more active when the presence of consciousness is experienced in the heart region. This process helps you to experience deeper emotional states of consciousness, with little active thought and greater enhancement of your emotional faculties. With the refocusing of your consciousness and energies in the heart region, you can further develop your intuition, reminding you of your purest innocence you had at birth.

Shoulders

- ◇ Cross your hands to touch your shoulders so that the right hand is on the left shoulder and the left hand is on the right shoulder.

- ◇ Keep your eyes closed and divide your attention equally on your shoulders.

- ◇ Take a resting breath.

- ◇ Sing *SAA* ending with a humming, nasal sound.

- ◇ Now take another resting breath and feel your presence in your shoulders.

- ◇ Move your hands to the next posture.

You need immense strength in your shoulders. A great amount of flexibility is required to perform the activity of motion. The strength and power is transmitted from the arms to the hands, so that they can hold, release or express feelings through natural gestures. This posture represents protection and shielding against invasion by outside forces.

Much of the strength to defend yourself comes from here, so this region needs the projection of your mind as you touch and pronounce the sound.

Elbows

- ◇ Slide your hands down so that you cup your elbows with your fingers open and your shoulders and arms relaxed.
- ◇ Keep your eyes closed and retain your awareness at the elbows.
- ◇ Take a resting breath.
- ◇ Sing *ROO* ending with a humming, nasal sound.
- ◇ Now take another resting breath and feel your presence in your elbows.
- ◇ Move your hands to the next posture.

Elbows are like feet as they are one of the most ignored areas in the body. Energy takes different forms in joints, changing from potential to kinetic. Usually you can see that the elbows of many people are rough, calloused and prematurely wrinkled. The elbow as a joint, like the shoulder and knee joints, contains important synovial fluid that lubricates the joints and is responsible for ease of movement. It is the eventual reduction of this fluid that results in the bones of the joints rubbing together and causing the condition known as osteoarthritis.

This occurs partly because the elbows are not well looked after, felt and embraced. As a result of touch being offered to the elbows, they become our treasure points and not just pressure points. Wherever you touch, Prana, or life force, flows more easily into that region, increasing vigour, vitality and beauty.

Hands Together

- Bring your hands together.
- Keep your eyes closed and be in the awareness of this gesture.
- Take a resting breath.
- Sing *GO* ending with a humming, nasal sound.
- Now take another resting breath and feel your presence in your hands.
- Move your hands to the next posture.

This is also the first yoga posture and a gesture of unity. It is the place from where the mind originated, like a lotus emerging from the lake of deeper consciousness. Once you fully experience this gesture, you will be reminded of your original innocence and purity. Your aura, or bio-conscious electromagnetic field, expands when you are absorbed in this gesture. While in this posture, you empower yourself with greater unity and focus, and everything appears to be in perfect balance.

Throat

◇ Place your hands over your throat.

◇ Keep your eyes closed and now bring your awareness to the throat.

◇ Take a resting breath.

◇ Sing *VAUM*.

◇ Now take another resting breath and deepen your presence in your throat.

◇ Move your hands to the next posture.

A gentle intended touch on the throat affects the thyroid and thymus glands. This can stimulate the body's immune response, which enables it to fight diseases and ensures optimal metabolic function. This may prevent allergies, arthritis and other inflammatory diseases. This location is like a conduit between the external and internal worlds. By becoming fully aware of your touch in this region, you can experience a sense of tranquillity. This position can help to improve the quality of speech.

Mouth

- Place your hands softly over your mouth.
- Keep your eyes closed and invite your mind to the mouth.
- Take a resting breath.
- Sing *SAA* ending with a humming, nasal sound.
- Now take another resting breath.
- Move your hands to the next posture.

Although the mouth is well guarded with strong teeth, in contrast, it also has gateways that are soft, tender and cushioned, as well as moistened, providing access to the tunnel of the mouth. These are the lips from which you utter, sing, eat, drink and express love. When you want to express good wishes and goodbye with affection to those leaving or going on a journey, you kiss your own fingers as a flying kiss and thus extend your feelings through touch. Here you offer a similar touch in a meditative mood and produce harmonious sound vibrations that have two positive effects, one from the touch and the other from sound energy reflecting back to your mouth and face.

This posture signifies saying less, doing more and expressing the rest in silence. Be mindful of what you consume. When eating or drinking, be guided by your feelings as well as by the sense of taste. This will help you to know whether it is good for you.

Nose

◇ Place your hands over your nose.

◇ Keep your eyes closed and invite your mind to your nose.

◇ Take a resting breath.

◇ Sing *ROO* ending with a humming, nasal sound.

◇ Now take another resting breath and feel your presence in your nose.

◇ Move your hands to the next posture.

A rhythmic sound produced in the nasal area can prevent or alleviate nasal and sinus diseases. The sound also stimulates the base of the skull, harmonising the hormonal secretions of the pituitary and pineal glands.

Cheeks

◇ Place your hands over your cheeks with the right hand touching the right cheek and the left hand touching the left cheek.

◇ Keep your eyes closed and invite your mind to your cheeks.

◇ Take a resting breath.

◇ Sing *GO* ending with a humming, nasal sound.

◇ Now take another resting breath and feel your presence in your cheeks.

◇ Move your hands to the next posture.

You are holding your face with great care and compassion, as if it were a diamond with many facets to it: your mouth, eyes, nose and ears, arranged artistically from the throat to the forehead.

Ears

- ◇ Place your hands over your ears, keeping your fingers and thumbs together.
- ◇ Keep your eyes closed and invite your mind to your ears.
- ◇ Take a resting breath.
- ◇ Sing *VAUM*.
- ◇ Now take another resting breath and feel the effect in your ears.
- ◇ Move your hands to the next posture.

This is another beautiful experience of your own sound-energy. You experience how it resonates and reverberates in your body. Your ears need regular touch which can increase your ability to concentrate and be more sensitive to distant sounds while in places of Nature.

Eyes

- Place your hands over your closed eyes so that your fingers are gently touching your eyelids.

- Invite your mind to your eyes.

- Take a resting breath.

- Sing *SAA* ending with a humming, nasal sound.

- Now take another resting breath and feel your eyes with the focussed touch.

- Move your hands to the next posture.

This touch is very important for your eyes. It is a challenge for us in today's world to look after our eyesight. Air and electromagnetic pollution bombard our sensitive eyes. Sound pollution, dust and stress also affect our eyesight. Medication and disease can also have a detrimental effect on our eyesight, for example in diabetes. When you touch your eyes, it is like connecting with the element 'fire', recognising and comforting the sense of sight. This organ is an extension of the brain; consequently, with this position you are creating a calming effect to the head.

Forehead

- Place your hands over your forehead, so that the fingers meet in the middle between the eyebrows.

- Keep your eyes closed and feel your mind in your forehead.

- Take a resting breath.

- Sing *ROO* ending with a humming, nasal sound.

- Now take another resting breath and enhance your presence in your forehead.

- Move your hands to the next posture.

This point is believed to be the 'Third Eye' where all the different types of energies of the body converge to become one. Meditating upon this location is said to bring about the unity of the individual mind with the cosmic mind. When you cannot think properly, you often touch your forehead, because you want to feel your full conscious presence there. This helps you to work better and to find solutions. That is why people often scratch their head unconsciously to find answers.

Crown

- Place your hands on the crown of your head.
- Keep your eyes closed and invite your mind to the crown of your head.
- Take a resting breath.
- Sing *GO-VAUM* at a manageable and stable high volume.
- Now take another resting breath and feel the pinnacle of the body - the crown of your head.
- Move your hands to the next posture.

GO stimulates the logical brain and VAUM the creative brain. Here you experience synchronicity, and thus enrich the nimbus around you, expanding your consciousness. This position helps you to be in balance, enhances concentrative ability and brings a sense of peacefulness. This is a subtle yet most powerful centre, a beautiful whirlpool of energy located above the crown of the head.

The head-organ/brain is like a control tower. This is from where our thoughts surface. Some thoughts are impulsive, some are intuitive and some are wilfully generated. At least to a considerable extent, we have the freedom to produce thoughts that will affect our life, the world and our environment.

Your touch will be very much needed to reduce harmful thoughts.

End with singing the complete sound SAA-ROO-GO-VAUM with the hands-together posture.

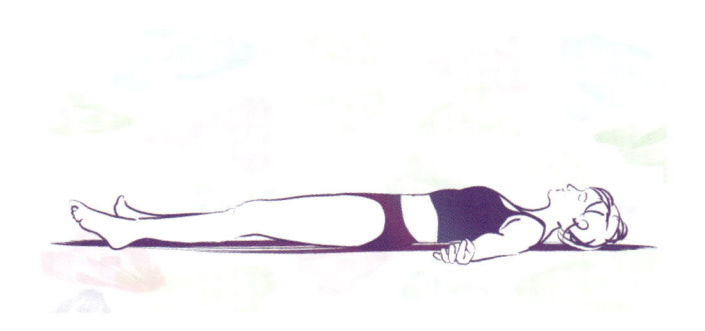

Yoga Nidra

Continue to keep your eyes closed and stretch your legs out in front of your body. Remove the cushion and place it within easy reach. Lie down gracefully on your back. Rest in this posture with your hands in Jñāna Mudra gesture and allow your body to become completely relaxed. Simply become an observer of yourself.

Feel the total weight of your body on the floor. Feel your body being in a state of complete rest. This is known as Yoga Nidra.

If possible, create the energy of these meanings in you:

- ◇ My body belongs to Nature. I now have no involvement with my body.
- ◇ My body is like a galactic dress provided for me, suitable for this part of the Universe.
- ◇ I am here only to experience myself in the body. The body has a separate entity called the soul and I want to experience the core-self/soul through the body, and eventually come to the realisation that I am the soul and I am everything.

You are taken to the realm of the serene heart-consciousness. There you do not perceive any difference in anything. Enjoy simply being in oneness and experience oneness in your being.

There is no time limit for the Yoga Nidra posture. It depends upon your personal need. You will be urged to wake up once the concentrated experience begins to recede. Keep your eyes closed throughout the entire process.

In Yoga Nidra, when you let go of everything unconditionally, you feel the infinity within, as you enter a stress-free world.

Yoga Nidra is a blissful state of Yogic sleep. You feel timeless and bodiless, experiencing great relief from the burden of the mind and the heaviness of the ego. In Yoga Nidra you breathe softly and subtly, and wake up feeling refreshed, (whereas sometimes after a deep sleep, in which you breathe deeply, you may wake up feeling tired). Sometimes thirty minutes of quality Yoga Nidra can be equivalent to hours of normal sleep.

Concluding

When you are ready to conclude, roll slowly to your right and rise back to the sitting position. Take a few deep breaths. Remain relaxed with your eyes closed for a few moments and enjoy the state of equanimity. Rub your palms together slowly to produce some heat in them. Then place your warm palms on your eyes and gently offer touch to your face and eyes. Open your eyes.

Now your hands are back on your knees, with a straight back and your head held upright. Slowly move your head to the right, and then back to the centre. Move your head to the left and back to the centre again. Then move your head to look up, and back to centre. Move your head down, towards the ground, finally back to centre. Unfold yourself from the sitting posture and it's time to stretch.

You have now completed Arka Dhyana IM. Remain in a contemplative state for a minute or so and gracefully return to your activities. It does not matter whether you go into meditation for a few seconds or for an hour. It is the quality of experience that matters - you will see the difference when you emerge. You may notice this especially more in classes guided by experienced and qualified instructors.

After IM

When you return to the surface of your mind and body, you feel relaxed and refreshed with renewed energy and new inspiration.

Refrain from immediately engaging in loud conversation as this is likely to quickly diffuse the peaceful mind, relaxed body and inspiration gained during IM.

With regular practice you will train your body to be in a state of motionlessness for a prolonged period without discomfort or pain. Perfect postures can cure some illnesses. If it is not possible to master all postures, master a few or one that is well suited and comfortable for you.

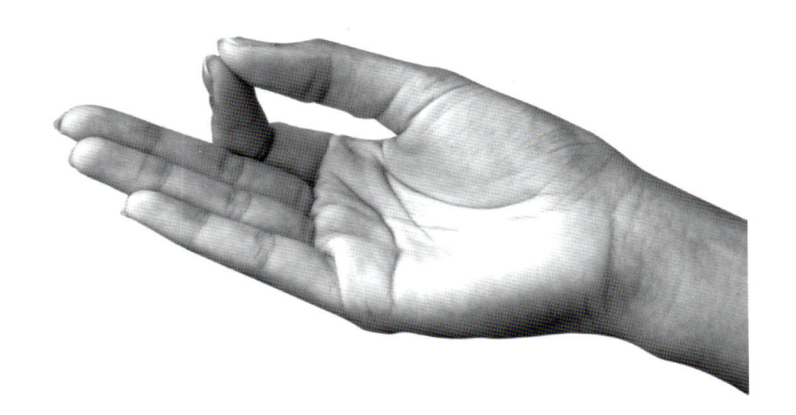

The Jñāna Mudra gesture

This special and most effective brief posture known as Jñāna Mudra can be performed in situations where time is scarce and you feel the need to make your intuitive voice brighter. For example, when you are stressed, before an interview, before an important meeting, or before you make a decision. In this circumstance, you can use this gesture to gain a positive impact on your mind.

In order to form the Jñāna (pronounced like 'gyan') mudra gesture, join your thumb and index finger together. Your other fingers point outward.

To experience the Jñāna mudra gesture on your heart, simply place your right hand (with the Jñāna mudra gesture) over your heart. This is a gesture indicating inner-wisdom. This is where your spiritual heart is identified with the Self. You can also form the Jñāna mudra gesture with your left hand and place your hand on your knee with your palm facing upward. (See the Jñāna mudra-heart posture on pg. 113).

Customising & Progression

As your practice evolves, you may want to vary your approach to the iM process. Here are a few suggestions.

Breath: Additional resting breaths may be taken before and after singing the sound at any point. This allows you to further unite with the point being touched.

Sound: If you are unable to feel your presence in a specific area, you can stay a little longer and sing the full SAA-ROO-GO-VAUM rather than just a short syllable, repeating the sound if necessary. Observe how the feeling deepens in the area you touch, and master your mind to invigorate and revitalise those areas.

At each touch point, you can sing the whole SAA-ROO-GO-VAUM in one breath, if possible. Repeat this for the entire process. This may be something you want to try when you know you have more time for your practice. You can practice without counting breaths, staying at each posture as long as you feel the need, feeling the benefit of comfort and connectedness. Allow yourself to be immersed in the experience of being at one with whichever position you move to, whether it is the knees, chest, forehead or any other.

*When you visit mountains, valleys, rivers and verdant land,
your first instinct is to close your eyes for a moment.*

*Take a deep heartfelt breath to admire and acknowledge
beauty, love, truth and serenity, which are
a reflection of Nature in us.*

Progressing

In your pursuit of IM, you may experience distractions and disturbances until you reach its critical threshold, particularly during the early stages of practice. It is therefore crucial to understand and realise that positive results grow with time and practice. The essence of success is action, which requires effort, which in turn requires discipline, dedication and consistency.

Different ways to say SAA-ROO-GO-VAUM

Any recitation, chanting or normal pronunciation of a sound like SAA-ROO-GO-VAUM, can be done in three ways. One way is to say it aloud, the second is to say it in a whisper so that only you can hear it, and the third is to recite it internally.

The effects vary accordingly. When it is uttered aloud, others around you also benefit. In whispering (audible to yourself), you gain physical benefits and spiritual benefits are derived when the sound is recited internally. You can implement this according to your own requirement.

IM with Nature

We should try to be in an atmosphere, environment or surroundings where we can access our deeper mind, our mother heart, our unconscious deeper Self.

Once you have mastered IM with the nineteen touch points, you can try practising with Nature, as the result will be more effective. When near the sea, sit on the beach during sunset. The gentle breeze will embrace you. Experience Nature's touch throughout the body, from the feet to the crown; experience the wholeness of touch by the breeze. Try to build up a rhythm in your breath to synchronise with the wave, like the dancing breeze outside - the breath of the Earth. The next stage is to become more conscious of the subtle sound of the breeze, as though it is singing to you with a message intended especially for you. Then project your mind to experience the sound of the ocean waves.

Become receptive to Nature's rhythmic sounds. Although they sound common to our ears, sounds such as the eternal waves of the ocean can provide specific spiritual information to individuals that are attuned to hearing it. Let your conscious awareness swing gracefully from the experience of touch to the experience of sound, and you harmonise your breath with the breath of Mother Earth's breeze.

Once you feel strongly that it is now time to become timeless and action-less, lie down on your back as the sun begins to set. Submit yourself totally, let go of everything. When you are under the infinite sky and very close to Mother Earth and Nature, bliss takes over. While the sound of the waves outside may seem to contradict the silence within, great harmony can be achieved. Stay until you feel ready to return to your mind and body-awareness.

Deepening the Sense of Hearing

Gently place the palms of your hands over your ears and project your awareness onto each ear. Feel the effect of your touch and how immensely sensitive your hearing becomes. While repeating SAA-ROO-GO-VAUM, alternately move your palms away from each ear. Feel the sound and touch and experience how conscious awareness shifts from ear to ear.

Experience this presence of your mind in a rhythmic but oscillating movement. You are teasing the sense of hearing, and enhancing this part of your concentration, while stimulating the sense of hearing with touch and sound simultaneously. This can help you to overcome apathy and develop the ability to comprehend abstract concepts. It can also have a healing effect on headaches and migraines.

This exercise and practice can enhance the power of your hearing. Your hearing may become more sensitive and you may be capable of focusing upon very distant faint sounds.

Rhythmic Touch

You can practice rhythmic touch at the end of your session on the crown of your head with your fingertips. Place both hands on your head and gently apply pressure from the fingertips, beginning with the thumb, the index finger and the other fingers in sequence; then in the reverse direction from the little finger to the thumb. Synchronise this touch with the rhythm of your breath. This rhythmic touch can be practiced at any of the nineteen energy points. It can be better learnt by attending any of the IM classes held in locations near you.

This can help you to feel the strong presence of mind, energy and the manifestation of conscious awareness in the area being touched. This may naturally enhance blood circulation, improving the flow of nerve currents, which helps to develop balance and increases concentration.

Connecting with natural sounds

When there is a thunderstorm, sit somewhere safe in a meditative position, bringing your full awareness to your ears and to the thunder. Nature's deep sound is highly mystical and soul-awakening. Our body represents sound. The body awakens from within, bringing its potential to the surface.

Experience the resonance of the bursting energy of thunder within you. The practice of becoming tuned and immersed in Nature's sound will help you to combat depression, fear and sometimes even aches and pains. The thunderbolt sound cannot be created artificially and effectively; you have to wait for the atmosphere to generate this effect.

We go about our daily lives without noticing or recognising such healing, soul-reviving and body-rejuvenating sounds.

Experiencing Touch Without Physical Contact

During the customary Arka Dhyana practice, you physically touch each of the nineteen energy points. In this advanced practice, you bring your hands to the energy points but, instead of making physical contact, you keep your hands floating about an inch above the point. You will begin to feel the experience of touch without actually making any physical contact.

This method helps you to develop more magnetism and healing ability in your hands. It enhances the self-healing ability of your own touch. You can become extra sensitive to energies and warmth around you.

Internalised Touch and Sound

This variation involves no actual physical movements as they are all internalised. The IM procedure is implemented internally. This method can be practiced in any of the postures as you evoke the stored coded impressions of each yogic touch. These impressions were created during your previous practice. You are now reviving them through internal stimulation rather than through physical touch. Although your mind may be occasionally distracted, with practice this will ease. Then, the experience of bliss begins. You enter a fourth 'state of consciousness', which is beyond the three normal states of wakefulness, dreaming and deep sleep. This state was named Avastha by early Yogis.

In recent times, mankind seems to be working against Nature, which in effect means we are working against ourselves.

We may not notice the effects now, but sooner or later they will become evident; the consequences are enormous.

Better results can be achieved by working with Nature more respectfully, then Nature will continue to manifest unabated, vibrantly for generations to come.

Arka Dhyana Postures: Quick Reference

1. Feet

2. Shins

3. Knees

4. Thighs

5. Waist

6. Navel

7. Abdomen

8. Chest

9. Shoulders

10. Elbows

11. Hands together

12. Throat

13. Mouth  14. Nose  15. Cheeks  16. Ears

17. Eyes  18. Forehead  19. Crown

Yoga Nidra

Gnana Mudra - Heart

Arka Dhyana Postures: Quick Reference

Questions and Answers

What is IM?

IM is a deep Intuitive Meditation (also referred to as Arka Dhyana) that takes place at the level of the heart, which is the centre of emotions and the centre of the body. IM reduces the pressure of mind and strengthens conscious awareness at the heart's centre. This brings profound insights about one's Self, including body awareness, and leads to the experience of different aspects of your being.

Why do we have to meditate and should it be an essential part of our lives?

Physical exercise is essential to keep ourselves physically fit. Similarly, we also should meditate in order to refresh and recharge ourselves. This will enable us to explore and experience our greater cosmic presence and positive potential.

We can live without meditation, but our ability to empathise becomes weaker and as a result, we become more mechanical, self-centred, selfish, and sometimes even violent. Also, we cannot connect well with other people, our latent creative and compassionate hearts cannot blossom, we may lack peace and the negative part of us begins to grow. We may become aggressive, apathetic, or depressed and as a consequence, general health may be affected. Without meditation, you will never discover how deep, special and magical you truly are.

Imagine the human head as the cockpit with the mind as the pilot of an aircraft. Here the mind must have full conscious awareness of the whole aircraft-like body. That is why IM emphasises the journey through the nineteen main whirlpools of energy in the body, by combining our own conscious breath, sound and touch at each energy point. This produces a feeling of strengthened unity within, empowering our body and mind.

Why do we focus on the body when performing IM?

It is difficult and unrealistic to keep focused on an external object for long. Instead, it is easier to bring your attention to your own body as you live within it. It is the shelter of your soul. Balance and a feeling of equilibrium is achieved by withdrawal of our mind and senses from the outside world. In Ashtanga yoga this is called 'pratyahara'.

Imagine that your body is like a transparent bottle filled with water, with a small bubble of air near the top which we can imagine as the mind. When the mind is prompted to travel through the nineteen points, you can imagine the transparent soft ball-like mind moving through each point you touch. The mind becomes simultaneously equally distributed when you touch both your knees, elbows etc. However, at individual locations like the navel or the throat, your mind becomes united again.

This exercises your mind and brain, dividing the function of the brain hemispheres into left and right, then combining them again. We can find a balance between logic and creativity through this practice, both are equally essential for our growth and expansion; any human growth and expansion contributes to the planet and to our environment.

Is lying down essential?

Yes, it is; otherwise the IM experience is incomplete. The upright touch sequence brings the feeling of physical unity, because it results in the pervasion of the mind throughout the body, enabling you to distinguish better between the body, the mind, and the realms beyond. Whereas the subsequent lying down sequence in Yoga Nidra brings about spiritual experiences, such as bliss, the after-effect of meditation. During the practice of IM, it is the contrast between engaging in a centralised activity in three ways—emotionally, physically, and thoughtfully—and then becoming physically and consciously inactive via Yoga Nidra, that prompts bliss to arise. When you awaken from this spiritual experience, you are likely to feel refreshed and elevated.

Does one have to be religious to practise?

Meditation is not a religious practice; it is a natural, universal activity that is free from any cultural, social, or other boundaries. You do not have to be religious to practise it. All IM requires is a receptive attitude and a willingness to conduct research in the laboratory of your mind and body, to reach enlightening consciousness.

Can I learn IM just from the published media?

Reading will help you to understand the principles and philosophy behind IM, which is your first step towards its practice. However, receiving training and learning IM practically, with an experienced and qualified instructor, will help you to learn it correctly and clear your doubts.

How is Arka Dhyana different to other methods of meditation?

Intuitive Meditation (IM) occurs at the heart level and helps the practitioner to journey from mind to heart. It does not involve mind techniques.

You use your own touch, your own sound and your conscious breathing.

Many say that they try meditation but cannot get the mind to quieten down.

In IM, the singing of the mystical sound, SAA-ROO-GO-VAUM, occupies the mind, as does touching the various points and breathing.

Because of this, many have found that there is less noise in the mind, and they experience more peace and unity within, enabling them to discover their intuitive consciousness. Later they have realised how this brings many positive results in their daily life.

IM provides a framework for practitioners to pull their physical, mental, astral and spiritual body 'layers' into alignment (harmony of mind, body and spirit) through focused direction of one's consciousness into different senses simultaneously. This is followed by a descent from the mind into the emotional intuitive heart, to journey into one's inner world, thus raising one's overall conscious awareness.

Employing this multi-directional approach subliminally keeps the mind occupied, helping to 'tame' its otherwise persistent chatter. Through simultaneous concentration on one's breath, and the formation of specific neutral sounds (thus avoiding mental images), as well as laying hands on specific energy centres ascending the body, the practitioner is focusing their intentions through the mediums of sound and touch. These self-generated activities contribute to an experience of 'feeling meditation' rather than 'thinking meditation', helping the practitioner to relax when they reach the zenith of the method. It is a whole-body experience, extending the body's innate healing potential to every corner of the body, resulting in raised conscious awareness of all that you are and indeed could aspire to be.

Physical benefits reported from this method include enhanced spatial awareness, proprioception and increased recognition of one's bodily presence.

Practitioners worldwide have testified to the self-development, relaxation and enhanced mental clarity offered by this unique meditation technique.

There is nothing more exciting, intriguing and inspiringly enlightening than studying, understanding and experiencing our own body, mind, emotional heart and inner self since we are the ultimate essential conscious substance representing the Universe in many ways.